The Bonds of Nest and Urn

The Bonds of Nest and Urn

Poems

Jefferson Holdridge

RESOURCE *Publications* · Eugene, Oregon

THE BONDS OF NEST AND URN
Poems

Copyright © 2025 Jefferson Holdridge. All rights reserved. Except for brief quotations in critical publications or reviews, no part of this book may be reproduced in any manner without prior written permission from the publisher. Write: Permissions, Wipf and Stock Publishers, 199 W. 8th Ave., Suite 3, Eugene, OR 97401.

Resource Publications
An Imprint of Wipf and Stock Publishers
199 W. 8th Ave., Suite 3
Eugene, OR 97401

www.wipfandstock.com

PAPERBACK ISBN: 979-8-3852-6132-1
HARDCOVER ISBN: 979-8-3852-6133-8
EBOOK ISBN: 979-8-3852-6134-5

VERSION NUMBER 12/10/25

You are the god who is lost—most boundless of clues!
Only since hatred scattered you across the ground
Are we true hearers, a mouth for nature to use.

RAINER MARIA RILKE, *SONNETS TO ORPHEUS*

Sure there are poets which did never dream
Upon Parnassus, nor did taste the stream
Of Helicon; we therefore may suppose
Those made not poets, but the poets those.

JOHN DENHAM, "COOPER'S HILL"

Contents

Next to Nature, Art | 1
Hands | 3
Truro | 4
Stretch of the River | 5
Early Successional | 6
Cottage and Stream | 8
January | 9
With Respect to the Nude | 11
Epic and Lyric | 13
On Caravaggio's Stolen Painting | 15
Proxima Centauri | 16
In Memoriam | 17
The New-World Firmament | 19
The Making of Snow | 20
The Works and Days of Art & Nature | 22
Song of the Projected Plane | 24
The Bond | 25
Nocturne | 26
The Child | 27
Human Frailty | 28
Birdhouses | 29
Greenhouse | 31
At the Pale | 32
Fishes | 33
Peace Lily | 34
English Ivy | 35
The History of Science | 36
Larousse | 37
Hawk and Cardinal | 39
The Deer and the Railroad | 40
White Oak | 42

The Oldest Testaments on Folly Beach | 43
Weather | 45
Weeping Cherry | 47
A Month Among the Seasons | 48
Wild Copperhead at the Zoo | 50
The Ballad of Spike and Seed | 52
From Another Country | 54
The Red-Tailed Site | 55
Plundered Houses | 56
The *Doni Tondo* of Michelangelo | 58
Sonnets in Search of an Object | 60
Sonnets in Place of a Subject | 62
The Secular Trees | 64
The Art of Balor's Eye | 65
Thirteen Resemblances | 66
Flora and Hypatia | 72
For a Weeping Cherry | 74
The Blank Signature (René Magritte, 1965) | 75
Art & Nature | 77
Nest & Urn | 78

Acknowledgments | 79

Next to Nature, Art

The art of nature or the nature of art.
Things, animate or inanimate, of potent form
Tell of the maker's hand, human or inhuman.
Born in nature, they grow to stand apart.
The marble, quarried and hewn, seems to warm
Enough to slay the giant. But what's done
With nature is not the subject. Nature will stay
Nature and yet itself become a poem,
In spirit if not upon the page, how stones
Remain stone but seemed designed to say
How stone becomes a statue of man or god,
How the sky becomes Brunelleschi's dome,
How the marble veil reveals Christ's bones,
And how fleet-footed Mercury is shod.

Nature as object becomes a force in culture
Until the two unite and seem the same.
But man is an animal, animal is not man.
Nature's a sibling, she is not a woman.
The difference between is more than just a name,
As metaphors of sea and stars may stir
Memories of passion and beloved eyes, inviting
The swirling water and looming clouds of self,
So nature conjures art to create the thing
No human hands yet made. There on the shelf
Or in the frame, the image beckons the herd

Which first inspired the horses on the walls
So two dimensions return to find the third,
For horses of illusion are feeding in their stalls.

Hands

Our hands are the most difficult to draw
Of all the body, but lovely to behold,
Whether figuratively or in the flesh
(Hearts are warm when hands are cold).
While in the arts they trouble every law
Of perspective as fingers clasp and mesh.
Sometimes on the table, they seem calm,
Uniquely ours, and then a finger lifts.
Or when the ungloved back turns its palm
Suggesting the dearest of all human gifts.

It welcomes another to read a life
Calloused from labor or soft from the mind.
Touch is a link between the bodily senses
And the theoretical. Art is rife
With tactile awareness. Sculpture designed
By hammer and chisel. Painting recompenses
Vision with texture. The hands that make
Conform to the hands they seek to wake.
Whether in paper, canvas, clay, or stone
The manufacture models flesh and bone.

Truro

Self-taught artist you had painted the sky
With a vertical instead of horizontal brushstroke,
But listened when the art teacher spoke.
The lighthouse looked solid. Its sharp border
And sun-washed blue distance led the eye
To disappear upward. There is an order
To the New England clarity of the scene,
Which brings me back years to Cape Cod
And those childhood vacations at Truro.
Later a national seashore, but then our cottage
Was perched among dunes we ran between.
Sitting here now, that seems so long ago.

You loved it there, but Mom complained to God
That all she ever did was cook and clean.
This was true, you later would acknowledge,
But the painting was done only twenty
Years after the war, and you, an ex-GI,
Having returned from Europe's theater of war,
Sicily, Naples, Corsica, bombers on high,
Had a new perspective but couldn't yet see
How nothing could be as it had been before.
The cottages would eventually have to go.
But your landscape of the lighthouse at Truro
Is next to our door, today left open wide
Upon a horizon, you'd now paint side to side.

Stretch of the River

Where the river is widest, it invites a crossing.
It seemed the distance created a need to be
On the other side, only to turn and see
The currents meet, where the waves' tossing
Suggests a bridge between future, present
Or past. Something like the Tappan Zee,
The earlier, evocative name, half Dutch
Colonial, half Lenape, to represent
Who hunted, fished, and settled, whose touch
Linked landscape, history, and perspective.

The crossing might have been pedestrian.
A three-mile walk by ships and pleasure crafts.
A place not merely to travel, but live,
Not a commuter rush, a string of rafts
To swim to and rest, while on shore a descendant
Of the Hudson River School adjusts her easel
Pausing over what the abstract meant
For the view upon her gessoed canvas.
The years advance and soon are gone, until
The bridge is renovated, the cars can pass
Upon this loud, polluted stretch of the river
And now she wonders what the scene can give her.

Early Successional

For Matthew Gaddis, in memory of painter Alexandra Zevin

The watercolors on the sunroom wall
Are all that remain of the white birches
We planted on both sides of the driveway.
An early successional, they seem about to fall
Already.
                    One is a stump, while another
On the left, the largest one, lurches
Out of the frame as if trying to say
That the bed of lilies of the valley
Amid birches standing like daughters and mother,
Curved leaves and bells, ladies of the wood,
White bark and delicate leaf,
Were never meant to last.

                      Yet they had stood
For a landscape that would outlive the wind
That eventually felled them,
                    Even she

Who colored the scene or we in our grief,
Observing them on the forest's edge,
Are early successionals, each destined
To die in the shade of the next generation,
Fostered by the unconditional pledge

Made for us, and by us in kind, one
For a future we will never be part of.

We bought a watercolor secondhand
Of white birches on a hilltop high above
A lake, caught at the peak colors of fall,
To match her summer birches in their stand.

One of hers was unfinished . . .
                      For suddenly the sun
Had moved and new images were made
As moments passed. "You cannot paint them all.
With watercolors," she said, "what's done is done."
The artist must be fluent in sunlight and shade.

Cottage and Stream

Gainsborough's women sit or step lightly
Into the prime of their beauty and out of reach
Of a poor landscape and portrait painter.
A desperate suitor with a long-handled brush
That trembled between limbs, eyes, and lips
Of women he could only vainly beseech.
A painter perhaps so smitten as to faint
There at the feet of models in dresses so lush.
One imagines the paint as it hovers and drips
Onto the canvas, before tormented he'd rush
To be among those as marginalized as he.
For after studying these rich young women, nightly
He'd go to the brothels, to those, like him, for hire.

Sometimes the expressions he draws from a sitter
Suggest a gentle understanding of his plight.
Perhaps sympathy, the simmering of desire,
However condescending, however dimly
Felt. Or merely just reflecting back the light
And shadow of landscapes he would always prefer
To paint. Thought to have changed the terms of sight.
Techniques that somehow "brought tears to the eye,"
Constable said, "and we don't know why."
Cottage and stream that set the world to right.

January

January is a two-faced monster
With Christmas behind steeped in nostalgia
And winter ahead between reluctance and dread.
The doldrums of the year without a stir
Except the fragile hope of falling snow
For cocoon amid the dormant and the dead.
A month of spiritual neuralgia.
But when the blanket spreads and winter's glow
Mantles to the sky, there is a deep
To which we descend that reminds us
Of how the temporal enlarges to its limit,
Not eternal yet, but as wakefulness to sleep
It borders between conscious and unconsciousness
And then moves beyond them both, to wit,
As Rilke said, poetry turns time into space,
But Janus is a god of double face.

So the poet is left to burrow in the hour
And finding nothing must search again with faith
That somehow, someway an exponential power
Will surface and fill the nearly empty page.
Torn, looking backwards and forwards, a wraith
Appears at some supplemental stage
Before vanishing like nothing else but snow.
The epiphany for Longfellow, Bridges, and Frost
Where Joyce's profane puts on a holy show.

Though angry Apollo ensures that hope is lost
In deep ravine there is a cross of snow.

With Respect to the Nude

If the beautiful were seen without their seeing
Us, without embarrassment or intrusion,
Without prurience or sense of being stalked,
Galatea might truly wake to being,
Where once she stood so perfect in illusion.
Pygmalion merely watch her as she walked
Or gaze along the avenue she ran,
Not coveting her because she was his own.
He might in quiet, pensive moments scan
Love and soul revealed as flesh and bone.

For her to be aware of this would ruin
The disinterested ideal of living beauty
Of polished marble below a gibbous moon
Made by hand or cast out of a mold.

But as the poet said, youth's tears are wild
And while she's young, the world is always old
And forgets to let the lovely grow up freely
Like innocence arising from the bath,
Or welcome them as any summer shower
That falls without the stormy signs of wrath,
Which woke the primal conscience of the child.

Who knows it isn't just wet fields in flower
Or a warm aesthetic gaze in which we bask.

For knowledge like an illness spreads distrust
Now Venus and Apollo wear a mask
To watch the mortal body fall to dust.

Epic and Lyric

The great white oak rises above them all.
When many are bare, its leaves shall hold
And seem to say that they will never fall
Until the tower knows, the time has come,
That neither the wind nor winter's cold
Could induce the tall tree so stoically dumb,
Even if leaves flutter and small trees flail
When in the darkest days the winds shall wail.
The tree is a gesture that only the light can change
Shining below or above from east to west
So shadows perspectives may rearrange.
Through hundreds of years, it withstands the test.
Though like its leaves it must lose its grip
And grasped while grasping its grasp must slip.

Dry brown leaves with austere beauty
Spin and settle on their deepening blanket.
Scratch and whisper sliding along the driveway
While across the street a smaller tree
Turns orange-red. A warm if brief display
Before our picture window, a jewel set
Among gray trunks, branches, and evergreens.
It answers with incandescent lyric form
The epic solidity of the great white oak,
Signaling a watch for the forest scenes,
How starkly quiet after last week's storm,

How in death something god-like spoke,
Of how in falling silent shapes could speak
Of what epic and lyric in each other seek.

On Caravaggio's Stolen Painting

There is a man and everyone knows him.
An outcast, poor and derided, with tattered coat

And broken nails. He often avoids the light
Like some animals. One of their own, he sleeps

Without a blanket in the cold. When day grows dim
Follow and you will see that he lives by rote

As saints do, praying morning, noon, and night.
Some suspect that he may be a saint

If not a murderer. A secret he keeps.
But Caravaggio has captured him in paint:

Once as *Saint Francis Alone in Meditation*.
Again as *Saint Francis in Ecstasy*.

And as a saint at the Nativity,
Seeking redemption because he is on the run.

Proxima Centauri

We cannot see what is too close or too far
But there Heidegger's centaur plays the flute,
    On electrons, or a half-hidden star,
        Pulsing proof of what we hope to find,
        Molecular life in distant galaxies.
Celestial music performed by unnamed lute
        Players who accompanied earthly songs,
        Composed in grief after a tragic night.

Masterworks of many hands left unsigned.
        No one knows to whom each piece belongs.
        Like the love that only appears as light
In Renaissance paintings, like the color
        Of Impressionist senses. Art's cities:
        The paradoxically natural premises of art.
        Columns like trees where lived the centaur

Till background landscapes came to the fore.
        Diaphanous perception torn by Descartes.
        Till the sun rises on legend, myth, and lore
And Mercury guides Cupid's random dart
        Across the lonely skies so it will soar
        Between the here and now and what's more,
        To transmigrate through death, to life and art.

In Memoriam

The lonesome whistles blow around the globe
From east, west, north, and south, trains
Signaling their passing, car after car after car.
As the mind awaits various thoughts to probe
Freighted with hidden cargo. Each sustains
The existence of the tracks they ride, clacking
Along in rhythmic motion, heard from afar.
The whistles are the knowledge of a previous age,
Both past and future, which memories bring
Of a technology turning page after page.
One that awakened the world to speed on land
As well as on the seas. Now flying through space
Wireless fidelity. You trust but don't understand.

It has taken time and made it a race
To outrun the mind, which once could imagine
What it could not build, but now can construct
What it cannot imagine. Da Vinci's ghost
Rides those trains from where journeys begin.
There he saw the cowboy hit by the truck
Passing from range to range, where a host
Of bison once roamed. Deep ecology
Before the idea existed. The City of God
Allowed wilderness and nature to be
Untouched, savage, alone in its evil and good.
No matter what, culture remains odd

Looking for our geneses out in the wood,
As weird and lonely as the spinning globe in space
Or a technology with which we cannot keep pace.

The New-World Firmament

Evening in mid-spring on a sunny day
And the tops of the tallest trees are lit
Like the expansive coasts and treeless hills
Your ancient landscapes span.

But here bats and swallows flit
Not merely circling the open sky
Which the wide horizon fills
On clear days, as far as the eye may scan
But where light and shadows play
And flocks of species fly
To tend or protect their nest
So no intruders find
Them. There's neither peace nor rest.
Raptors on the wing, snakes in the grass
The heart rattling in the breast.

The season, month, and hour must pass.
They linger only in the mind—
The canopy, the forest firmament—
Wondering what the symbols meant
By outward shapes and inner forms designed.

The Making of Snow

When there isn't the slightest breeze
The snowflakes gather on each
Tree after the leaves have fallen
And so they trace those lines
That almost seem to reach
The pendulous clouds.

The snow
Collected on limbs defines
A randomly cross-hatched sky
So that who sees will know
The exact space from here
To there, as though birds fly
To write an intricate pattern
Of flight, both far and near.

Once marked, we discern
After it's been snowing,
Just before it's muddy,
The wind's begun blowing,
That this was but a study
Of a final work in progress
To capture every shade
Black, gray . . . colorless
And will disappear as such,

Though the drawing snow has made
Is lit by every shining touch.

The Works and Days of Art & Nature

The four seasons form a crucifix
From solstice to solstice.
The equinoxes cross between
Height of the sun, length of day
Long or short, the vertical
And horizontal.

                Each one's a scene
An ever changing set and play
Of month's unfolding weekly scripts
That never finish, that is, until
One morning brings a tale to tell
When not one minor actor slips.

Yet most every month must swell
With references that do not match
And walk-ons and walk-offs, which
Are holes in the plot to patch.
Patches making motley. To stitch
Is the best that we can do.

                Seasons,
However, mark a rhythm and a cycle
To return to, symbols of aging,
Even of youth, in winter,
And hours in which we may be still.
Seasonal beauties are almost reasons

For the struggles of approaching
A whole we finally only splinter
Between the longest days and shortest.
The cross we bear and bend below.
Among the spheres a sense of rest.
The sun will keep the earth in tow.

Song of the Projected Plane

Carolina wrens know things that we
Will never learn though if we listen long
Enough perhaps we'll reckon why they sing
Beyond the science.
                    We named the chickadee,
The other songbirds, for like the human song,
Given an air and words, they appear like spring
Leaves and flowers budding as shadows fill.

Mystery demands so much repetition
For the sound to make sense. It eludes the will
To understand why or even how it's done.
Perhaps at dawn or sunset when each bird
Declares desires, boundaries and something
Else we feel, because we have often heard
The poetry, the lyric, as Whitman knew
The loved songs the mockingbird could sing
Together were a color, make it blue.

The Bond

As summer began by the banks of a stream
The twilight grew deeper and fireflies
Flashed in shadier parts of the field. She readied
Herself to catch the first of the year, her eyes
Fixed on air, awaiting the next bright beat.
She became the symbol of the evening and the deed
Of the season, appearing with warmth and twilight.
For she and they were highlighted by the heat
Expecting day's end, disappearing with night.
And signaling erratically in the sunset sky
That before sleep and passing far beyond
The horn and ivory gates, we meant to capture
Summer's enveloping warmth, what pleases the eye,
Akin to the deepest peace and keenest rapture.
Swayed by the elaborate rhythms and the bond,
Finite, we must imagine what lies ahead
Sealed in transparency, pulsing in jars,
Without limit, for us and without us, led
By numberless sands and generations of stars.

Nocturne

When the eyes shut for sleep
Is an absolute moment or world.
In closing, sight becomes two-
Dimensional. Height and width
Without depth. Blackness
In a room sealed tight
Will barely fade or surrender
Its shapes. A wall so steep
We fall in fear—hurled—
And abruptly break through
To find ourselves amid
Landscapes that possess
Abundant, mirrored light
That only night could render.

The Child

On the bottom of the sea, lights play
In shifting squares that match the surface
Waves, reflecting the sun in motion.
The two levels mirror, but only blend
At night—fractured every day.
Across the stones, an intricate lace
Of moss has grown in broken sun.
Subconsciousness will never end
In search of what is always missing.
The seafloor fissures. The water's wild,
As lava makes titanic war
Until it hits the surface hissing
Of currents, tides, the changing shore.
The waters break and bear the child.

Human Frailty

After Salvator Rosa's painting L'Umana Fragilità

The pestilence that swept through Naples
Took your family, but spared you and your wife.

The least pain you could feel was to weep
While writing a letter or as you would paint

The Angel of Death, a skeleton, taking the life
Of your son. Other children blow bubbles.

One feeds or catches a hummingbird. In faint
Colors, the silent mother struggles to keep

Her vigil. You painted your initials on the knife
That shed the blood, depicted slowly to seep

From all flesh. It is now difficult to see
The falcon of life hidden behind Death's wings.

Death guides the son to write of human frailty
On his mother's lap, who watches and clings.

Birdhouses

The one you notice least is the same
Color as our house to which it's attached.
Pure white, small. Birds who come are tame
Compared to most. Their temperament matched
To yours, present, friendly, and unafraid.
It's one of two houses we haven't made,
Which came with our dwelling, and the chickadee
Each year makes a nest there. We hear the rustle
In early spring as though it scratches at our wall
To remind us inside that there's an outside world.
It's always the first nester that we see.
There is contentment in light of summer's pull.
Having weathered winter, spring, and fall
We imagine a branch, the fledglings wings unfurled.

The other house stands before the window
And there we've watched the wren's long tail
Flick, and heard the many songs he sings,
Forty they say, but all of them we know
Are sung before the small bird spreads its wings.
Like the chickadee, he will not fail
To arrive and view our presence as familiar
As though we had met many years ago,
And had forgotten to regather until now.
He is that open, that curious, and sure
We have no designs on him. How that's so

Is a trick either of nature or of culture.
We do not know the why, what for, or how,
But are glad for what our houses will allow.

Greenhouse

Luxuriant through spring and summer
The leaves of potted plants have browned,
Yet their flowers will cling and stir
In autumn winds with little sound.
Afternoons when the sun is bright
Promise more warm weeks ahead,
Though one cold evening or early morning
Signals that soon there comes a night
Perhaps with just a sudden warning
When heavy frost will leave them dead.
They depend on us to watch and carry
Their tropical roots inside our home.
Like lovers, we'll lose them if we tarry,
But in the end there isn't room
For all. Only a greenhouse poem
Spares the tender shoots from doom.

At the Pale

At dawn, when the sun is low,
Sending you out into the world
Feels like broken trust.
For safety means to exist
Inside our house and yours.
On damp winter days I know
That the metal will rust
If left outside, the flower unfurled
In January will die in frost.
Each day the cows are missed
In their rolling brown field.
We want them lying or standing
On all fours, embossed
On earth like patterns on a shield.

Fishes

A tissue paper wind-sock of a fish
Conjured this poem about fishes.
A mold, or a handmade painted dish,
Imagined a seascape of wishes.

So here is your poem of a fish
Not of a fish, but about one. It vanishes
Into the waves from the hellish
Heat to a white-wine sauce, a sprig garnishes

The sea bass or the grouper, a knish
On the side, or better, butter varnishes
The fresh catch (this is becoming a niche
Poem) and everyone relishes

The chance to partake, except the fish
Who'd rather swim away. Delicious
Or not, the poem is like the fish.
It is no more than what embellishes

The fine palate, the mouth-watering wish.
The pond is empty but I think I heard a swish.

Peace Lily

Sensitive to drought within a week
It droops below the vase's edge. Watered
It freshens in an hour, shiny leaves
And arching stalks, even its hooded flower,
Which rarely blooms for us, slightly bends
On long and narrows stems, rises as quickly
And completely as it falls. It's like a gauge
Of what we notice, what we miss, and how
We treat the present world. It is as if
It knew we need reminding just to look
To see, never to be dulled by habit
Or lose ourselves in yesterday, as if
Its delicate nature were formed in sympathy
With what feeling had brought it as a gift.

English Ivy

Quickly spreading shoots,
And infiltrating grass.
You have to clip its roots
Before the vines amass
Climbing shrubs and trees
Standing in its path.

The exponential growth,
The fury of such math
Is fit for topiaries'
Neo-classical order.
All gardeners are loth
To let it breach the border.

I've seen it grace the cover
Or pressed inside the flyleaves
To ensure the poems would live
In those who can discover
In someone who conceives
How, when it is invasive,
Versed they come to be
In rampant English ivy.

The History of Science

Carried by wind, water, or ice, and "zeroed"
Of the sun's rays, the flaws in the quartz
Will hold the ensuing sunlight. When the stones
Are buried by centuries of shifting terrain
They await their discovery, found or bestowed,
Fossils of light, dormant seeds of sorts,
Till carefully grasped in darkness where they've lain
With earthenware, animal and human bones.

Then "optically stimulated luminescence"
Will tell a story of how elemental
Fire, air, and water were captured in earth.
How the tribes moved east to Salisbury plain
With their standing stones, so heavy to pull
Their source of belief, thither and whence,
Aims and origins, symbols of worth
Taking forms of worship, gestures of giving.

The quartz records the orbiting sun overhead.
Woodhenge was a place for the living.
Stonehenge a monument to the dead.
Once Orpheus could move the stones and trees
Now we silently make known our presence,
Unlocking secrets in their most ethereal sense
Of light, the naked eye no longer sees.

Larousse

What makes a bird a bird? Not only flight
But feathers, for bats can fly and they
Are furred, though flying without sight
They circle the darkness to detect their prey,
While dawn and dusk birds declare their part.

Thought superior to reptiles, inferior to mammals.
Like reptiles, birds have scales on legs and feet,
Lay eggs. Like mammals they have warm blood.
Their aortic arch in a four-chambered heart
Ascending the body, inclining to the right.

Snakes fear the bird that lands and trammels.
All animals fear the silent and the fleet
Raptors who can kill without a fight
And leave bones lying in the mud.

****

The exceptional feature of the bird skeleton
Is how the forelimbs are modified for flight.
Strange that some birds can only run.
Grounded, can they ever finally rest
As passerines do upon their perch?

Some birds weave, some convert their nest,
Hollow it out and hope the deed is done.
They call for warning and feeding,
Uncertain if they'll dodge the hunter's search.
They sing for territory and breeding.

Or sing because there's nothing else to do,
But give form to rain clouds and the blue.

Hawk and Cardinal

For Meghan McGuire

The sole red feather speckled with rain
And blood lies as if placed on the gravel
In your studied close-up of the scene.

The droplets are various shades of red
According to the blending of the stain,
Making the still life cruel, fast, and lean.

Happily, the hawk had returned, you said
Then mentioned cardinals, six in all
That had nested near your mountain home.

The hawk stooping through the sunlit dome
Struck and the cardinal struggling in its fall
Bequeathed its feather to the frame and poem.

The Deer and the Railroad

Nineteenth-century Russian writings viewed
The train as modernity's ugliest sign,
While Soviet dissidents would conclude
Trains were authoritarian and malign.

For both, human and animal had to die
Trying to cross the tracks around a bend
Or somewhere unsuspecting along the steppes
Or guilty, felt their condition had to end
And asked the train to beg the question why.

In America, trains are the rattle of the past.
The whistle of nostalgic lament that accepts
The presence of a treacherous crossing,
That the metal out of which they're cast
Bears the weight of oppressive symbols.
That the hammer and pick again will ring
Out prophecies that chance fulfills.

When the buck was wandering the city
It seemed an image of wilderness
Lost in its descent from the mountain.
It elicited wonder and prophesied pity.
She who saw it did not begin to guess
That this magnificent, powerful creature
With its pedicel, fork, and crown tine

Would lie dead, but unmarred along the tracks.
And in her childish imagination feature
As myth grown stronger when it succumbs to facts.

White Oak

Towering dangerously and with indifference,
On quiet days it's silent, but if it spoke
We would hear, for we notice every creak
It makes in the wind. Another out back
Also stands in mute dominance.
We know "the breaking of so great a thing,"
As Caesar said, "should make a greater crack."
So we listen for either one to speak
Admiring when the leaves begin to change.
Sometimes gusts seem to make them whistle and sing.
Their long, heavy limbs ramble and range.
Giants above us from the primeval world.
Some mornings out front, we find a branch that broke
And feel that an earthbound nature spoke
Reaching to the sky, unconcerned with us below,
That from far regions, a gauntlet had been hurled.
But we could only see the great white oak
With knowledge it does not care for us to know.
One we would not even understand
Because we are untethered from the land
While its roots grip and will not let it go.

The Oldest Testaments on Folly Beach

The beginning is like the end. The Pelican
Represents us to ourselves. Like other
Animals, we are exhibitions at the zoo
Of character, as they are *ad hominem*.
St. Francis knew it all, saying brother
Sun and sister moon. Anyone who
Lives beneath them where the planets run
Sees an unknown course vanish in the blue.

The fiddler crab waves its outsized claw
In a dance to woo a mate or warn
Off a rival. Obedient to the law
Of music that rules us all.
If that claw breaks in battle the other will
Grow large while a small one appears where
The outsized broke. Life's miracle is there.

The sandpiper is like a child playing
In the surf. It moves in sporadic bursts
According to a mood, it seems. Half rings
Of sea foam come and go like firsts
And thirds of a piece directed by the tide.
Whatever food it follows evades us all.
The view, the viewer, and bird are occupied
By the ocean's symphonic rise and fall.

Pelicans scour the waves like a squadron
Of cargo planes from World War II.
Those flying crates that did not have a gun.
But deftly they dive into the ocean stew
For each had then become a fighter jet
Built to explode on unsuspecting fish.
Their beak and pouch are like a spear and net
Or like a fork and regurgitating dish.

The first time we saw one standing on a pole
It looked so awkward we questioned, would it fall?
With a flap, it showed us it could fly
Not only well, but fast and powerfully
With heavy landings like an ancient soul
That had heard a distant god-like call
Finally to learn the how by wondering why.
It contemplated coasts like open texts,
Which blind prophets might memorize to see
The primal in what the present world reflects.

We saw this when we found the horseshoe crabs.
One intact though dead and facing the ocean,
Another emptied by countless hunger-driven stabs.
The work of carrion feeders like gulls is done
To Old Testament preaching: vanity of vanities.
The horseshoe, primeval descendant of the seas,
With a soldier's helmet, a weapon-like tail,
Ends by traveling to where it had begun,
Where the land struggles and the waves assail.

Weather

The most ethereal of all aspects of nature,
More object of art sometimes than art itself.
It is the subject of its own objective
Mood. In its everlasting stir:
Surf on the shifting continental shelf.

Like an artist it depends on forms to live,
Creates conditions of harsh or pleasant worlds.
It holds the calm that comes before the storm,
Then gathers in crescendo like a tragic
Drama. In English, it is a conjunctive pun
That turns on earth's angle and unfurls
Whether it's sunny, rainy, cold, or warm.
In extremis now, our watery planet's sick,
Though at a golden distance from the sun.

This week it shifted seasons in a day.
Here on the north-south line of Carolina
One season keeps the other one at bay.
The mountains to the west seem to define
A finger of the north that's pointing south,
But like the weather points without a hand.
Like winds from a disembodied mouth,
It disappears like paintings in the sand.

Whether earth weathers what we've done
We cannot answer. Weather will be free.
Creation that eludes the maker's hand,
Like a child's unleashed balloon or kite.
Weather will outlast the earth and sun,
But unlike Ariel when Prospero departs
The long affair with wind, water, and sea
Will be loveless, without life or light,
Without anchor and banished from the arts.

Weeping Cherry

If ever a name was a poem in itself
Weeping Cherry is—a melancholy eros.
It seems in the grandeur of the forest, an elf
Of hanging branches, flowers pink or rose,
Was planted by an errant gardener
To match the willow's weepiness,
Yet dangle its flower.

It has grown ancient in a Shinto shrine
In the worship of nature. Fountains of spring,
A poet's tree, unlike the laurel's crown
Of renounced desire and humanity, a divine
Emblem of our mortal selves, swinging
Loose and delicate, pulled down
By gravity, but making it a source of grace
To weep in such color.

                          Early to flower,
To leaf, and very early to lose its leaves,
Branches breaking in the wind. A shower
Of leaves or petals. We struggle to trace
Its limbs as they thinly drape in sheaves
Above the azalea and the rhododendron.
Leafless they stand to show the poem is done
Till orbits change and new poems have begun.

A Month Among the Seasons

Sitting in the sand beside the shore
The fleeting days of August seem to move
Like distant ships across the endless water
Set squarely before the background of the sun.
They look as though locked inside a groove
That runs along the edge of the horizon.

A watchful Greek had seen the ships sail over,
First the mast, the prow, and hull appeared.
The earth was round. The galaxy sun-centered.
In heat and light, as autumn's darkness neared,
Metageitnion burned bright, yet labored toward

A month among the seasons and the line
Between one season's progress and the next.
The flowers, leaves, or snows become a sign.
The recto/verso reading of the text.
Pliny notes that when the crickets sing
You have approached the summer solstice.

Antony was dead. Three realms had been at war.
Civilization shifted with Augustus
As Roman peace descended after slaughter.
The month he named fulfills the hopes of spring.
Though mad King Lear banished his best daughter,
Odysseus returns and inland plants an oar.

The geese have not begun their clamoring
Some leaves have turned, birds begun to stir.
Now the crickets rattle in the mind
That once were only a murmur and a whisper.
Unlike December, August fires through
The feeling that the summer left behind
Glaring in the sky to shroud the blue.

Wild Copperhead at the Zoo

What's in
a place?
What in
a name?
The fixed
& telling
eye, motion-
less as death.
When seen
outside
the frame
of the dense
forest floor
where sun &
shade overlap
as they pass
in their race
to where
the bobcat
freezes at
the railing,
not because
of snakes
behind
glass
but the

wild
copper
head
half
off
half
on
the
trail.

The Ballad of Spike and Seed

> Pronunciati da quella voce così gradevole avevano per lei un suono nuovo, e se li diceva dentro: Ardito, Tibisco, Mentana, Saragolla, Taganrog, Gentilrosso... Gesù, non ci ho mai pensato prima, ma che bei nomi tiene il grano: so' più belli di tanti nomi di cristiani. Ma come va che a qualche cavallo suo Giordano non ha mai messo il nome di un grano?
> —Maria Orsini Natale, *Francesco e Nunziata*

Why were those grains of semolina
Given such names as Tibisco,
The legendary Taganrog, Saragolla,
Mentana, Ardito, Gentilrosso?

For the list has a poetic pull,
But memory comes with remorse.
The names of the grains so beautiful
They should be the names of a horse.

That they grew in the Ukraine was odd
Why wouldn't the Italians grow better?
As the spike of the grain was their god
And they followed its laws to the letter.

But the stuff of the harvest is fickle.
It changes with weather and soil
In the years of the sower and sickle
And the days of backbreaking toil.

It's the seed that determines the grain
Its flavor is hard to retrace.
The child of the sun and the rain
Like culture, language, and place.

So amid the famine of war
The destruction of acres of tillage
The weight of the hunger they bore
The survival of plunder and pillage

They ate all of the Taganrog left
Until after, it could not be found.
Italian pasta bereft.
The legend no longer was ground.

So the ballad of spike and seed
Ended in lands of the North.
The harvest succumbed to the need
And never again would spring forth.

From Another Country

A series of destinations safely reached
Despite hurdles, detours, threats, and crimes,
Haunting memories even if forgotten,
Guilt or hurt that cannot be impeached,
Or cleanest page that shows the trace of grime
Exposed to air.
                Ripe degrades to rotten.
So the journey bears the weight of origins
And ends, driving and impeding—as though
In refrains of contradictions there begins
A set of limits that must be safely breached.

Once before two thousand years ago
The camels brought myrrh, frankincense, and gold
Along an astral and planetary path—
One we hope that someday we will reach.
The zodiac reveals, as the story's always told,
An infant to beseech.
An algorithm that eludes the terms of math.

The Red-Tailed Site

The hawks that hunt along the banks litter
The watershed with the bones of their dead.
The winding course of the Yadkin's muddy water
Is linked by networks of indigenous sites
And the age-old paths they travelled.

Between villages there was a recurrent flow
Of nature into culture. These ancient rites
Tap the springs and rivers of the world
In flood and drought, which bodies deeply know
Brings water to water, dust to dust, flesh
To flesh.
        We watched as the lithe dancers unfurled
Their limbs throughout the river's length, to mesh
With its reflections, suffer its pollution, question
Its damming then moved, so still the waters run.

Plundered Houses

Some are never inhabited. Perhaps
They are not angled right or too near
To brambles, tree, another house, or nest
Or too unstable. Once left, they seem to lapse
Into oblivion as places that bring bad luck.
We've left them where we put them. Each year
Thinking they may yet be a fitting host,
We know that they provide a place of rest
Or in winter's wind a cover in which to tuck
Oneself until the storm has passed. We fear
That many birds may give up the ghost
To predators, snakes, raccoons, or owls.
Most of our houses have survived the test.
Each entrance the most distinct of vowels,

Which signals songs but also midnight howls.
When a house was torn from its tree at night
We woke to find it by the broken shells
Scattered on the ground. A sad sight
We vowed not to repeat. A bluebird
Had built its nest there and lost its young,
Like a farmer who confronts his empty wells
Or a shepherd who cannot find the herd.
We longed to see and hear the song he'd sung.
The house we had provided had been plundered.
This year we would be more diligent

And ward off the raccoon with the scent
Of garlic, to keep the vampires from the door
As from our child upon the upper floor.

The *Doni Tondo* of Michelangelo

Did he turn to painting with the thought
That poetry's tools are like the hammer and chisel
That the stone contained the image to be wrought
As sentences are shorn of fat and gristle.
For he made the stone the theme of his lament
That sin would always mar the image copied
Splitting the world into a message sent
From God, the Dove, the Holy Spirit's seed
That still it would be lapidary work
To find the truest thought where it might lurk.

The hewn and polished line of stone divides
The profane nature of the ancient world
(Embracing nudes among the rugged boulders)
The sacred drama of the family curled
Around the power of the "mighty mother,"
The potent Infant, lifted on her shoulders.
An altar in a circle marking sides.
Pater thinks the cultures are combined.

John the Baptist in his animal skins
A forerunner who is like a brother
Where the Advent violently begins.
The Baptist in the wilderness would find
A voice to herald the merciful answer

To Oedipus.
                    St. Joseph's scandal meant
That earth and sky would merge in the ascent
From John's eyes to the Virgin's.
                    The Devil screams
Among the tendrils within the gilded frame
For Christ above will bless the wedding dreams
As though to fulfill and refute them were the same.

Sonnets in Search of an Object

On the screened-in porch in the backyard
Off the kitchen. One story up in summer
Looking over the two-acre swamp and pond
Where leaves played scales in the animated zephyr
Like one the Greeks had given a soul beyond
Nature. A setting in contrast to the hard
Narrative that hit noon and unfolded after
In the quiet when birds are falling silent
As they stay until evening, and after the dawn
Chorus. Frogs, cicadas have yet to croak and chirr
When a deer might graze upon the lawn.
The stillness of midday will capture the moment
The story (despairing beauty) would slowly begin
More about tragedy and less concerned with sin.

Though culpability is sustained across the ages
From childhood to adulthood, for women and men,
One episode condensed the many pages
Turning through the last century's strife.
But I could not understand it then,
A four-year-old arriving at St. Vincent's
On a cold, rainy day in late November,
The alcohol, job loss, attempted suicide,
I would remember it later as my parents'
History and as my father's life.
When biography narrows, history opens wide.

The measure of man is never his lot.
Unlike that visit, or the Epiphany he died,
The day I heard was all the story was not.

The pang would linger until the summer evening.
The realization of the unrelenting struggle
Neither won nor lost. Hope against hope.
How much had gone awry and how long
Was I not aware? Scene after scene
Like a Greek drama in which freedom followed
Necessity as necessity had freedom. A family's wrong
Became the burden of conscience to stay with us still
Demanding its object, but which one has the scope?
Boulders or lilies lining the driveway that face
Our house or cumulous clouds in mind that flowed
Across the sky on those days when we read
In sun and shade of a time and place
Free of yet true to words our mother said,
The feeling within moving swiftly overhead.

Sonnets in Place of a Subject

The sky resolves into a deeper hue
Saying nothing that we might understand,
As though it were opaque and yet see-through,
As though it were a riddle of the things
And not the things themselves. Sky without land.
The sun's motion as it seems to pause
The bee that's known only by its stings.

At the highest latitude, it is the blue
Of twilight and night-shining clouds.
The essence of nature's arbitrary laws.
Each one absolute in cause and effect
Remains convincing yet forever shrouds
The art that we freely would elect
In solitude, but which is lost in crowds.

The air is its own apparent meaning
More than merely sound, the lyrics form
A grammar to cast a spell and something stirs
Leaving listeners hushed already gleaning
That what they can't explain is a live and warm
Enchanting spectral room where it avers
But never makes a statement. A great refusal
To take sides, with no moral ambition.

Pure sympathy comprehending all.
In place of any subject, every cognition
A version of the song to woo its mate,
Happy when the poem finds its young,
Yet sad at the prospect of their fate.
Its only purity that the song be sung.

The Secular Trees

The changes are so imperceptible they
Require secular time to witness
Growth the trees resolutely sustain.
We notice how tall they have grown,
How wide, as though only yesterday
They were saplings, but we have known
Bramble that grew season to season
So thickly, we would have to cut
It back like other errant weeds,
Which in the survival of the fittest
Would quickly overrun the garden.

Last autumn was the year of the nut.
This year the nuts became seeds
(When not hoarded in the nest
Of squirrels), then budding oaks
In tended beds there to profane
The gardener's work, which as such
Comes to view each fertile breeze
With suspicion. The rain soaks
The ground. The sun wakens too much.
For every invader we may seize
In our labor we must remember
That amid the grove of secular trees
And bleakest days of dark December
The sacred extols the gardener's touch.

The Art of Balor's Eye

Jutting with the angle of my vision
Bouncing between the eyelid and the lash
The floaters circle falling through the sky.
The medicine swims across my eye
Smarting from the diamond knife's incision.

As binoculars might focus on a bird
A rifle's scope lock upon its prey
A mind search desperate for a word
Igniting when it finds the one to say
A volcano is ready to erupt
Smoking for decades until the soldiers land.

They shoot across the crater like a bow
Trapping those who do not have a hand
Who still can see the strategies disrupt
The images from rightly filming how
The retina is emblazoned in a flash.
Perhaps the clouds will billow in the sky.
The heavens fill with slowly swirling ash,
As the world explodes under Balor's eye.

Thirteen Resemblances

Nature has given us
Metaphors to link
Ourselves to its gifts,
Allowing us to think
Beyond "because" and "thus"
Through an image that lifts
Us to our poetical
Beginnings. The very same
That Vico outlined as "mythos,"
Language born of shame
And thoughts metaphorical,
Which artists must disclose
For nothing lacks a name.

The color of the leaves
Are those of the hawk,
Squatting among them
Spreading its wings,
Then preening on the swings.
His talons like a stem.
While the crows squawk,
Silently he watches
For resemblances
To make them his,
As an artist might

To take off or alight.
Sovereign in sight.

The carpenter bee
Though fearsome looking
Is harmless. Still, to see
One startles at the initial
Presence, buzzing. No sting
But it bores holes
Into wood so round
They look artificial.
Its deliberation extols
The search. When one's found
It seems to assess the size,
Enters, or is elsewhere bound,
As though art had its spies.

An artificial goad:
As the cars go by
The pollen and the leaves
That gathered on the road
Are swept up and fly
Down after them.
Some are solitary.
Others roll in sheaves.
An occasional blossom
Suddenly seems to flee,
Scrambling all alone—
A poet who would be
Like a rolling stone.

Does a possum play
Possum or does it freeze
In fear where it might lie.
Whatever the game, it loses
Should a car go by.
Be better if it flees.
But what being chooses
How to act in the face
Of death, which till then
Is faceless. To assert is to play
Possum, exactly when
Reason has left the place.
Then what does the artist say?

Moving prisms of
Light on paper and wall,
Floors and furniture.
Fragments of rainbow whirr.
Sometimes the patterns stall,
Sunlight clouded above
The solar battery
That sets the crystals in motion.
Rhythms difficult to see.
Speeds too varying
Like a flashing ocean
Or notes too lively to sing
With syllables lingering.

Though less than five feet tall
He handled a basketball
Like a pro, and yet
Every second shot

He'd take, we'd block
Though he'd set at the spot
He'd won horse round the clock.
We were very happy
Every time he was able
To visit. His aim, with luck,
He said, was to be
"Thirteenth at the table"
Quoting *The Wild Duck*.

"The devil it is," he'd forget
That last line of the play.
Idealism with realism met,
As on that destined day
We chose Barabbas not Christ.
Is art a fatal idealism?
Like religion, certain to stir
What it can't satisfy?
Inspired and hindered by nature,
A temporary prism
That slowly directs the eye
To covet what enticed.
The ideal sacrificed.

And so, we plant a garden
To avoid the devil's hand.
Sweet William in a ring.
Desert plants for when
There's a drought. Planned
Over the course of years.
Glorying in spring, holding
On in winter, in summer

Cherishing those that sustain
Themselves with little rain.
Planting in the chirr
Of crickets' failing desire
Still burdened by the fire.

Annuals and perennials
Continue a conversation
That has no beginning
And knows no end.
It promises an "until"
But delivers only "for now."
For that's decided by the sun.
We have only to tend
The relationship between
Death and resurrection.
The time that we allow
Or are allowed unseen.
The future is seeded right now.

Today I planted an azalea
Between roses and liriopes
Then nestled a begonia
Near aging evergreens.
The first sits by a sculpture
A head with closed eyes
Imagining different scenes
Beyond the architecture
Of house, garden, and trees.
Another of art's spies
Through which humanity sees

And refreshes itself to think
As birds in a birdbath will drink.

Tomorrow awaits the next
Day, the next thought,
As a reader follows the text
Unsure of what is sought
Until the options are few.
The aim and end clear.
The resolutions rarely new.
The suspense a suspended fear
That only drops on cue.
What is the sound we hear?
What bird has just landed?
Or was the mockingbird taught
A song from elsewhere stranded?

And what do we know of it?
What of its future or past?
Will the metaphors last?
If no one understands
The sounds of bird or poet?
Or will resemblances surface
In other forms, a grammar
Rolling like unmarked lands
Or like echoing weather
From afar, a trace
Unseen, half-felt, half-heard
There in the tone of a word
Or memory relayed from the hands?

Flora and Hypatia

In a small house on a hill beside the sea
Long ago, almost two thousand years,
Flora was born to a life not meant to be
More than one of service, of constant fears
And love for and by others, family
Prevailing as it would as long as tradition
Did as well, at least in some form, diminished
By the strict expectations of history
And freedoms that over time were slowly won.
Latent in Flora's birth, Hypatia rose, fished
From a river, and being golden, was set to be.
But in the beginning, it could not be done
All roles were arranged, a burden to be born.
An object of veneration and subject of scorn.

One day she went outside to gather flowers
In a white gown, her hair pulled back
And lightly crossed Primavera's green
A painter saw and wished he had the hours
To do her justice, though perhaps the lack
Of time forced the moment to be seen.
For in the minutes he had, as Flora stepped,
He sketched the act so ably the artist
Knew that this fresco could be his best
In angle, contrast, color, style, and concept
And felt that then the pressure was the test
To consider the subject, the nature of the lack

The two robes, a basket, the turn of the wrist.
A season's matter captured from the back.

When does a culture turn from war to peace?
From sarcophagi covered with scenes of battle
To philosophers at table on life and death
From Homer's *Iliad* to Jason's golden fleece
To study from a Trojan's dying rattle?
And are the changes transient as a breath?
The armor is buckled, or artworks reappear
Books are written or cities are destroyed.
Is the moment of symposia or agora
Merely a prefix or a suffix of the fear?
That the vandals are only elsewhere employed?
They'll soon invade to take the likes of Flora
Carrying the vase or emptying the wine
Vessels broken in purpose and design.

Once the frescos inside the sarcophagus
Instructed the dead, like the famous diver
Launching into the unknown or like the women
Weeping over the dead. Why do they cry?
The departing souls must ask as they pass by
Reflecting on the many lives of women and men.
How much of existence lies on each survivor
As he or she struggles toward refinement and thus
Remembers the artist who created the threnody
Hoping the body once corrupted would free
The spirit beyond the measure of words
Which compose the constitution of an age
Beyond the farthest migration of the birds
That Flora would be Hypatia on the page.

For a Weeping Cherry

Now a memory lingering in an empty space.
A veil removed from the flower bed
That gives surprise to the house's face.
For it sees everyone as would a nude
Suddenly looking at the viewer, like Manet's
Olympia when the model turned her head.
The not ideal first critics thought it rude,
But our cherry adorned a milder gaze
Since moving here and shall be missed.
Strange that the year the tree had died
(As though the time had come to insist)
It had more flowers than many springs before,
Or was it, as often, the season knew and lied,
So once blooming the tree would weep no more.

The Blank Signature (René Magritte, 1965)

Woman on horseback riding between
The trees in a dense forest when our eyes meet
Her looking slightly to our right. It seems
That she is painted on a tree. An illusion.
Yet the background appears in front of the horse.

Perspective in the Renaissance, of course
Is paramount, aimed to extend the beams
Of light shining from a window. This light
Being God's by which we see and feel.
Subjectless landscapes leave us in flight

Looking for meaning in the background
Where colors are signatures of seasons. Autumn
Gold and summer greens. A raised hoof
Of the horse suggests a future sound
That doesn't come. A heatless sun

Must be shining although it's unseen.
The intricacy of brushstrokes, the warp and woof
Of tapestry when there isn't a thread.
Everything is visible, everything between
And exactly painted as the hat on her head,

As if the imagination could only exist
In the title, the blank signature, the twist

Which binds me to the variation of style,
The sense that art glows with the spirit
As it eludes the mind by fooling the eye.

Not cleverness for its own sake, but wit.
Not the trickery of the avant-garde,
But the height of myth, religion, art.
The best ending where the best should start,
By making a mark as a diamond is hard.

Art & Nature

What ties the black snake to his prey?
Besides fear and hunger. What links the canopies
To the earth besides the matching roots?
What moves the planets in their solar orbits?
Besides gravity. The strength of the sun
Must represent something beyond its ray.
A source somewhere other than where it sits.
The taproot must suggest more than the trees.
The hunt mean more than the gun that shoots.

A river of forms in which we dip our hand
To find the given and made are constantly met.
And when all is thought and said and done
The invisible ligature between art and nature
Inextricably binds them, like the ampersand
Where "per se" is indistinguishable from "et."
The Latin etymological metaphor
One gives to earth, neither sea nor land.
A sculpture for memory not allowed to set.

Nest & Urn

When Landor writes, "next to Nature, Art"
Does he mean lesser, as many think
He must, or side by side, each a part
Balancing the whole, on the brink
Of union, art as nature or nature as
Art, the universe by design, a nest.
Blueprint to reason why the maker has
Formed what artists model or contest,
And seek to know what secretly was planned.
Plinth and purpose on which the artworks stand.

Seeing that the water ran fast and clear,
Who were the first to lean over a river?
To use a hand to drink, the first to mold
The clay to carry water when they were not near
A source, who saw a natural depression
And then searched for the best matter
To shape, which was strong enough to hold
Long enough to last a generation.
Stone, iron, silver, plastic. Gold,
Ancient, precious, holy from the first.
So take this cup, nest of Lord and Son,
For flight and landing, memorial and thirst.
Nest and urn, eggs and ashes, life
And death, striving toward the end of strife.

Acknowledgments

Dedicated to my friends and family, far and near.

"Hands" is from *Poetry Wales*, How I Write (online series, Spring 2024), https://poetrywales.co.uk/jefferson-holdridge-how-i-wrote-hands/.

"Truro," "Stretch of the River," "Early Successional," and "Cottage and Stream" are from *The High Window* (online), https://thehighwindowpress.com/2025/03/04/american-poet-jefferson-holdridge/.

"Human Frailty" is from *Asheville Poetry Review* (print, Fall 2024).

"With Respect to the Nude" is from *Poetry Ireland Review* (print, Fall 2024).

"Fishes" is from *The Christian Century* (print, Feb. 27, 2022).

"On Caravaggio's Stolen Painting" is from *Poetry Wales* (print, Nov. 2025).

"For a Weeping Cherry" is from *The Galway Review* (online), https://thegalwayreview.com/2023/09/15/jefferson-holdridge-four-poems).

www.ingramcontent.com/pod-product-compliance
Lightning Source LLC
Chambersburg PA
CBHW061502040426
42450CB00008B/1453